Published by G. Whizzard Publications Ltd.
in association with André Deutsch 1977
105 Great Russell Street, London W.C.1.

Fact Books © G. Whizzard Publications Ltd 1977

Text © John Amis 1977

No part of this book may be used or reproduced in
any manner whatsoever without the written permission
of the Publisher.

ISBN 0233 96770 2

Printed by Dainippon Tien Wah (Pte) Ltd.

 G. Whizzard/André Deutsch

The Facts about a Symphony Orchestra.

Featuring The London Symphony Orchestra.
Introduction by André Previn.

By John Amis
Photographed by Philip Sayer

Series consultant editor: Alan Road

Introduction

If I were to make a list of the books to which I would be qualified to write the introduction, that list would be pitifully short. The other day, at my favourite book shop, I glanced idly at some of the books geared to the education and edification of children, and realised that by no stretch of the imagination could I write any words of experience or wisdom for volumes entitled "Your First Book of Wildflowers," or "Pottery at Home," or "Fun and Profit through Beekeeping," or "Everybody's Favourite Minor Welsh Poets." It was a blow to my conceit, I can tell you.

So therefore, when the publishers of the book which you are now perusing asked me for a brief foreword I was relieved to see that, at last, here was a subject on which I was qualified to speak, not just on one, but on two counts. Here's why: not only do I spend most of my life working with symphony orchestras, but I also have five young children at home!! You can imagine my elation. My children, ages one through six, are, perforce, surrounded by music. They are used to seeing their father sit in corners of his study, making mysterious markings in large scores. They are accustomed to musicians bringing over strange looking cases, unpacking them, taking out instruments and producing noises thereafter; and they are blasé (for their age) about wandering blithely about the backstages of most of the major concert halls on two continents. I often think that their first words must have been "dressing room", "rehearsal" or "airport", all of which have almost equally pertinent meanings to the professional musician, as you will see in detail when you read the text of this book.

Through the media of concerts, recording sessions, and television, my children have had a ceaseless curiosity about that strange animal known as the symphony orchestra, practically since the day they were born. They have asked me probably a million questions concerning the orchestra, what makes it tick, and how and why it is possible for so many

men to share the same goals at the same time, work so terribly hard, and yet have such a good time when they finally produce beautiful music.

However, all these questions, even if they were multiplied by a large number, would not scratch the surface of the detailed and loving information in this volume. Of course it is true that *any* symphony orchestra of world repute could have been successfully used for a model for a book such as this; but it so happens that the author has seen fit to use the orchestra I like better than any other in England, the London Symphony Orchestra, or, as it is familiarly known to most people in the concert world, the LSO. This gives me one more advantage, because it means that it is *about* my professional "family", and *for* my real family. Actually, although the text is so clear as to be instantly comprehensive to a child, it is also so knowledgeable as to be of instant interest to anyone of any age. I have seen a great many explanatory books which, in their eagerness to be palatable to children, have substituted lovable bears or revolting bunnies for the actual thing, and have drowned in their own cuteness. Well, Mr Amis has not stooped to that gambit. No, he tells it straight and true. He does not minimise the glamour of the actual concert and does not underplay the reward which great music can give its performers, but he has also concentrated on describing the hard and even harsh life of the orchestral musician. He is a professional himself, so when he speaks of life on tour, and the endless problems of making ends meet, and schedules mesh, he knows whereof he writes. The chapters on rehearsals, on tours, and on recording sessions are both witty and documentary, and his look around the instruments of the orchestra is as detailed as anyone could wish, be they six or sixty.

I am grateful to this book as a conductor, as a playing musician, and as a parent. I will buy five copies and distribute them around the house. Come to think of it, I will get six and keep one for myself.

André Previn

Life in the Orchestra

Playing in an orchestra is on the whole enjoyable. At its best it can bring a feeling of well-being and joy that borders on ecstasy. The knowledge that you are sharing that feeling with 90 people adds something mysterious and extra to that joy—sometimes the orchestra will 'take off', do something that hasn't been rehearsed but is right, almost the way a flock of birds will suddenly wheel one way or the other.

The men and women in the orchestra also have the feeling that they are doing what they have been trained to do, are doing it well, and are giving pleasure to other people by doing it.

But the rewards, gratifying though they may be, don't come easily. Playing in an orchestra, particularly one of the top orchestras in the world like the LSO, is very hard work; the hours are largely anti-social and the pay relatively low. And unlike most occupations, the job carries no pension.

If there is lots of hard work for the orchestra, there's also lots of variety. Included in the almost non-stop schedule of rehearsals, concerts, recording sessions, and television appearances are regular trips to the provinces and overseas. This can mean London, Edinburgh, Brussels and Luxembourg one month; Japan and Korea the next.

It must be said, however, that their journeys to foreign parts are not always as glamorous as they sound. The conditions under which the orchestra performs are as varied as the audiences it plays for. An unheated, dilapidated Korean school-hall in winter is a far cry from the air-conditioned comforts of the Festival Hall.

Quite often one of the LSO staff will go in advance to spy out the land in respect of hotels, meals, and, especially, the seating in any unfamiliar halls. Sometimes the hall will not allow the usual placing of the orchestra, and unless the conductor is very quick on the uptake he may find himself for the first half-hour of so bringing in the horns when he should be beckoning the cellos. With any luck the horns and cellos will spot his error!

Overseas tours can have their funny moments. During a visit to Japan, there was a brief but very loud earthquake noise in the middle of the night. Everyone dashed out into the courtyard at the front of the hotel, only to see the tuba player leaning out of his fifth floor window, saying, "Sorry, fellows, it must have been something I ate."

An orchestra is really no place for someone that likes to lead an active social life. There's not much time for hobbies, or going to the theatre or cinema; not much time to go out with the wife or husband, or look after the children; not even much time to *practise*. The chances are that the player will be too tired on his evening off to be the life and soul of the party at home.

Yet, surprisingly, nearly all the LSO do have interesting hobbies; in addition many of them teach, passing their experience and expertise to the young. Most of the orchestra are also very aware of the need to keep fit in a life spent sitting playing for six or nine hours a day, and try to do something about it. The average age is about 37.

Whatever the demands, the job clearly has its compensations. You won't find the LSO a depressed, frustrated bunch of people. Not as a rule. Travelling to exciting places helps. But the main factor in keeping them resilient is the power of the music itself.

It's difficult to explain why exactly—in fact, if you could explain the power of music to lift up the heart and the spirit, perhaps music would lose something of its power, its magic and healing properties. At any rate it is that power that makes an orchestra tick; provided that the conductor knows his job and that the music warrants replaying (music that is all colour, gimmicks, or emotionally shallow, soon palls).

Mind you, don't expect the LSO players to come out of a session looking like a saint in a film who has just had a peak experience. After a good concert you might hear from them, "that wasn't too bad", or "I think X (the con-

factbook/LSO

ductor) is finally beginning to learn what it's all about", or, more likely, "what about a drink?"

The LSO

The LSO is proud of the fact that it was formed as long ago as 1904, twenty-six years before the first of the other surviving orchestras of London. (BBC 1930, London Philharmonic 1932, Philharmonia 1946, Royal Philharmonic 1946.)

London has five major orchestras, which means that the competition is keen; whereas the rest of the world's best orchestras operate in towns where there is *no* competition: Amsterdam, Boston, Cleveland, Milan, New York, Philadelphia. Pundits keep on saying that two London orchestras ought to be eliminated; if this happened the LSO would not be one of them, because it is one of the best two.

There have been many conductors of the LSO during its long history. Hans Richter conducted the first concerts but made no records. Arthur Nikisch made some historic records with the orchestra in 1912 before taking them on their first American tour; that was an occasion on which the LSO nearly foundered.

Owing to last minute alterations, the management switched the orchestra's sailing from the *Titanic*—which hit an iceberg and sank, drowning hundreds—and travelled instead on the *Baltic*, where the worst that happened was a concert in heavy seas, mid-Atlantic, during which the oboeist was sick in the middle of a solo.

The composer Elgar was much associated with the LSO over many years and recorded with it. In modern times the chief conductors have been Josef Krips, Antal Dorati, Colin Davis, Leopold Stokowski, Pierre Monteux, Istvan Kertesz and André Previn.

Edward Elgar · Josef Krips · Pierre Monteux
Istvan Kertesz · Leopold Stokowski · Antal Dorati

Revenue

During the year 75/76 the LSO played:
- 126 concerts
- 236 rehearsals for concerts
- 148 sessions (TV, records, film)
- a grand total of 510 playings.

Of the concerts, 39 were put on by the LSO itself; for the other 87, the orchestra was engaged by an outside promoter.

The LSO generally makes a loss, sometimes a large one, on its own concerts—even if it is a sell-out at the Royal Festival Hall in London. This is because the revenue from ticket sales simply does not cover the basic rehearsal and administrative costs.

Where the LSO is engaged by a promoter, however, it usually makes a profit; the fee charged adequately covering all the expenses. Why then doesn't the orchestra try and get more of these engagements?

The answer is that, in most cases, the programmes for these concerts are 'popular' rather than 'prestige', with the LSO not having choice of conductor, soloists or programme, and having to make do with only one rehearsal—not enough for really good playing. There are exceptions, such as the Promenade concerts or those organized by the Royal Philharmonic Society, festivals, and so on.

The LSO gave only 26 concerts in the rest of Great Britain, the remainder taking place in London or abroad.

The amount of money the orchestra receives from engagements is chicken-feed compared with the sums earned from recordings for films, television and gramophone records. Unfortunately for the orchestra, it gets no money in the form of 'royalties' on records (only a fee for playing)—the conductor usually does, so does the soloist. One per cent for the orchestra would balance the books.

After all the revenue from recording contracts and other engagements has been added up, the LSO is still in the red. To help pay the deficit the orchestra gets a government grant—Arts Council money administered by the London Orchestral Concerts Board; each of the four independent London orchestras (but not the BBC) receiving approximately £140,000. In addition the LSO gets financial help from Peter Stuyvesant, the cigarette manufacturer, and from various other business concerns, including British Airways.

But the arch enemy inflation has shown itself to be no respecter of good music, and with constantly rising costs the orchestra's struggle to make ends meet becomes more difficult each year.

Administration

Like all the other London orchestras except the BBC, the LSO runs itself. All the players are shareholders of the company and they elect nine directors who decide what shall be done. These directors sometimes meet in the LSO office, often between rehearsals or sessions, sometimes in backrooms, railway trains or hotel bedrooms, or even, recently, round a lamp-post behind the Albert Hall. Being a director means giving up quite a lot of time, even some of those precious free days.

The day-to-day administration of the orchestra is handled by a small staff, headed by the Managing Director. Apart from the latter, the key people in this group are the Concerts Administrator, the Publicity Manager, and the accountants.

There is no pension for the members of the LSO when they retire since each job is paid separately: no concerts for a week, no money. But there is an annuity scheme, a poor substitute but it's better than nothing. Non-playing members of the LSO staff receive a straightforward salary.

The orchestra owns no instruments except for the percussion and a celesta. But it does have its own van with driver, and Robert Cornfoot.

Robert, who is the porter, knows all the ins and outs of every hall and studio that the LSO visits, as well as customs regulations for the foreign tours, and how to cope with getting the gear on and off airplanes. He handles the delicate instruments in their cases with the greatest possible care, and before a concert or rehearsal sets out the orchestra and puts up the music stands.

Another permanent member of the LSO staff is Graham Waghorn, the Personnel Manager. Graham's job is to make sure that the orchestra is complete and that any extra instruments that may be called for in the composer's score are there when required. Some works, some types of concerts (Bach, Haydn, Mozart, maybe 'strings only') need less players —all this has to be sorted out. Similarly, one

work in a programme may need many more players than the rest; it can be boring for the 'extras' to attend a rehearsal where their work may not be played, so the personnel manager keeps everybody informed.

Graham is also responsible for seeing that the players are in their seats 'at the ready' for rehearsals, concerts and so on. He needs a good resonant pair of hands to clap together: "Come along now, gentlemen, PLEASE." He is the stage manager, so he also makes sure that conductor and soloist(s) make their appearances at the right time.

Library

Another possession of the LSO is its library (housed in the Royal Albert Hall, together with the celesta) of orchestral scores and parts. In charge of the thousands of separate pieces of music is Henry Greenwood.

The LSO library.

Robert Cornfoot, the LSO porter

One of the chief things in a performance is to get all the various strands of sound together, all the members of the departments either breathing or bowing in unison. To achieve this the orchestral parts are marked accordingly, showing the players where to breathe, or where to change bow (up or down). Modern works contain more details, but most of the composers of the time of Schubert (1797–1828), and before, did not usually put in instructions of this sort; nor, very often, much information as to how long or short certain notes should be, or whether a phrase should have the notes detached (staccato) or tied together (legato).

If half the orchestra plays a tune one way and the other half the other, it is going to take time for the conductor to find out what is happening and adjust things to his satisfaction. Communication can be difficult. Many of the players are seated some way from the conductor; some of the conductors mumble, or can't make up their minds, or speak English indistinctly. Which can all take up valuable rehearsal time. Multiply one such correction by 50 and 3 hours would go with only 10 minutes of music rehearsed.

Which is why the individual instrumental parts are marked in advance, usually by Henry Greenwood from master copies prepared by the conductor and/or the leader. The majority of conductors will adopt 'standard' bowings and breathings, but there are always exceptions. And over and above that, a conductor like Leopold Stokowski is convinced that string players should all bow at different times so as to give a better continuous sonority; in other words, he likes everybody out of step! (It sounds wonderful when *he* conducts but his method doesn't suit everybody.)

So Henry looks after all this and, in addition, sees to the hiring of orchestral parts that the LSO does not own: with a great deal of modern scores the music publisher finds it better business to hire parts out, rather than sell them.

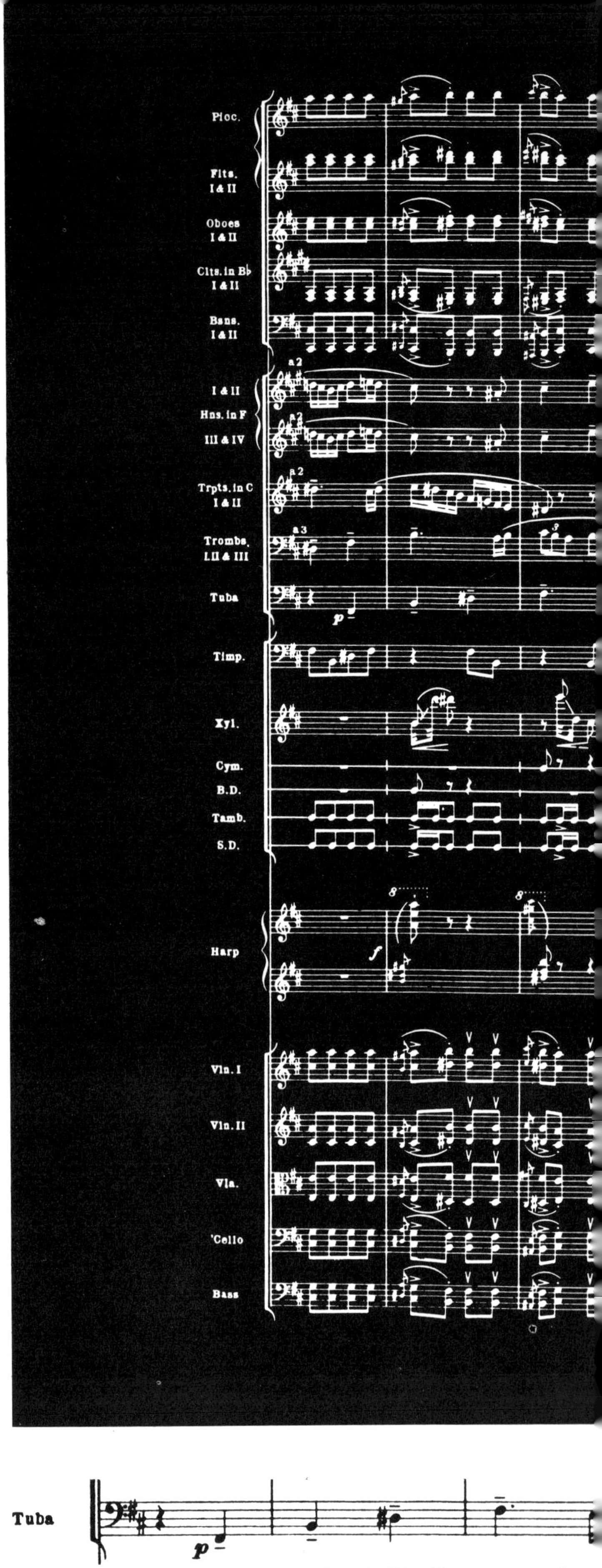

Part of the score from Benjamin Britten's 'The Young Person's Guide to the Orchestra' – with the tuba part from the same secti

© Copyright 1974 by Hawkes & Son (London) Ltd.
Reprinted from Hawkes Pocket Score No. 606 by permission of Boosey & Hawkes Publishers Ltd.

Conductor

Who needs one? Well, there was once an orchestra in Russia in the 1920's that had no conductor. It soon packed up. And for two main reasons: firstly, all the players had to be able to see each other, which meant they had to face inwards and the audience could not hear properly; secondly, and more crucially, it took for ever to rehearse.

Up to the beginning of the 19th century music was not so complicated; with his bow, the first violin could give the lead to his (by comparison with now) smallish orchestra and this would work. But with orchestras of 80 or more, this has become far too difficult. Conducting is a full time job, and needs two hands.

The principal function of a conductor is to interpret what a composer has written and bring it to life through performance. Music notation is fairly accurate but not entirely so; it is not enough to print the notes, the speed at which they are to be played, and various other instructions. Music played strictly in time is deadly dull, as witness pianolas (mechanical piano-players) and the records and tapes of recent synthesizer music. It bears the same relation to real music as a waxwork model does to a person, or a wig to a real head of hair.

No, it is the subtle gradations of rhythm and phrasing, and the ability of the conductor to mould the shape of a piece of music, which makes it potent and moving. A string quartet (two violins, viola and cello) can achieve a good performance by working together for weeks and weeks on one piece; the LSO can do it in two or three rehearsals.

The conductor is the only person in the orchestra who has the full score in front of him during a performance; the instrumentalists having only their own parts written down for them. This means that the conductor has to read instantaneously and simultaneously 20 or 30 lines of music. Of course, he prepares this in advance, but there is always a time when he has to conduct something 'at sight' and he wouldn't be a proper conductor if he couldn't do this.

The conductor Josef Krips claimed that he could teach an intelligent teenager the actual 'beating' gestures—how to start the orchestra, give the tempo, keep it going, stop it, bring in this or that section—in three-quarters of an hour. And Antal Dorati has said that there are only six basic things to say to the orchestra at rehearsal: "louder, softer, faster, slower, longer, shorter." But there are certain subtleties.

At a rehearsal, the LSO once queried the actual loudness of a certain passage marked in the score 'poco forte' (directions in music are often given in the language of the composer, but more usually in Italian—a convention dating from 300 or more years back to a time when Italian music dominated Europe—thus poco forte, 'a little loud'). The conductor, Pierre Monteux, twinkled and said to the cellos, who had the tune, "poco FORTE" and then said to the violas who had the accompaniment, "POCO forte." This is a typical example of the printed musical directives not being complete enough; it is also an example of the perfect way, simple and smiling, of dealing with an orchestra.

In the 19th century when there were no unions and no government grants to orchestras, the players were very often treated harshly by conductors; they were the bosses and had the right to hire and fire the men. Conductors would talk about an orchestra as 'their instrument', as if they could play on it as they would on a piano. Even today there are some who still believe in the 'Divine Right of Conductors' and, if they are sufficiently respected by the players, they may get away with such autocratic beliefs.

But heaven help the man on the podium if he thinks he is better than he is! A professional orchestra can tell within five minutes whether a new conductor is any good or not, and can be merciless if he doesn't come up to scratch.

Most younger conductors try and steer a course between being too familiar and too aloof. Many of the players will be on Christian name terms with him, but not all. It's not easy to maintain the right balance and all too easy to sacrifice respect.

A conductor has to know his music and his scores, know what the orchestra is capable of, collectively and instrument by instrument, and know that necessary amount of stick technique —the rest is *will-power*. Will-power and know-how make that indefinable difference between: the word from one teacher who can tell you to do something and you do it happily; and the same word (spoken just as loudly or softly) from another teacher, and there's no way you're going to do it.

These days it is usually the orchestra that has the power, as the LSO does, of hiring and firing the conductors, rather than the other way round. And yet, paradoxically, the LSO loves a conductor with great authority, provided he gains their respect and can make them play within an inch of their lives. There are not many of these super-conductors in the world today, where we all strive for equality.

In some ways the LSO seems like a bunch of musical lions looking for a tamer trainer. They are quite temperamental collectively, and once they have learned one repertoire of tricks they may want to dispense with one trainer and find another. Thus, every few years the orchestra may find it wants a new conductor or a new management. This is to the good in many ways; it keeps things fresh.

In earlier days, and in some places still, the conductor of an orchestra directs nearly all the concerts in the season; but the LSO does not operate that way. It has found that the relationship with a conductor works better if they don't see him day in, day out; and vice versa. So, André Previn conducted only 47 concerts (out of 126), 6 records, and 6 television programmes during the 75/76 season. Others conducted the rest.

This arrangement works very well because Previn is best in the more colourful romantic and modern repertoires. The other conductors employed in the season were mostly specialists in the classical repertoire.

There can be no doubt whatsoever that the LSO is on the crest of the wave right now; and it owes its position to a number of factors. Management of the last 15 years has been variable, but on the whole it has given the orchestra the right prominence, enough work, and a good image. The choice of conductors has built up the standard, virtuosity, and level of playing. Krips and Dorati gave it solidity and brilliance; Monteux gave it elegance; Stokowski sonority; Kertesz romance and ebullience.

André Previn has many of these qualities but perhaps his chief claim to fame has been to bring the orchestra to a wider public. In Great Britain, Previn is 'Mr. Music'. This is, of course, mainly because of his gifts as a conductor, composer, pianist, musician and communicator; but there is also his youth, his ability of getting through to young people, his association with jazz, and so on.

Inevitably, all this brings some reaction from amongst the establishment, intellectuals, even at times from the orchestra, who feel perhaps that getting through to the young isn't everything. But André Previn's contract with the LSO means he is only there half the year (for much of the rest of the time he is principal conductor of the Pittsburgh Symphony Orchestra in America), so the orchestra can find other conductors to complement the image.

In the meantime, let us hope that the great work of the LSO and Previn goes on and that they continue to give us more marvellous performances of Berlioz, Tchaikovsky, Richard Strauss, Rachmaninov, Walton, Prokofiev, Vaughan Williams, Stravinsky et al. . . .

When Herbert von Karajan conducted the Berlin Philharmonic Orchestra in London in 1976 he was paid as much as the whole orchestra—£4440. That's big money, and only Leonard Bernstein is in the same league. Their annual incomes are probably around £250,000, maybe more in the case of Karajan who con-

trols a veritable empire, with interconnected contracts for television, records, films, operas, concerts and festivals. Bernstein's income is probably less now that he no longer has a permanent orchestra of his own.

But this whizz-jet-baton-biz breeds: managers, accountants, private planes, the best suites in the best hotels and all that sort of thing. At a performance Karajan has one man to hold his coat or a wrap, another waiting with brush and comb, and so on—they're known as 'Herbie's coat-hangers'. Bernstein's aides include one man whose job is to have a lit cigarette at the ready, so that the Maestro can take a quick puff when he comes off stage between bows. (There is also a well-known violinist who butters his ego by insisting that the car that takes him from the airport to the hotel is always a white Rolls-Royce.)

As American politician Adlai Stevenson once said: "Success is all very well as long as you don't inhale."

Sir George Solti, Karl Boehm and Carlo-Maria Guilini are the other three of the *top five* money earners among the conductors. After them comes a bunch of world *superstars*; their diaries are full for the next 7–8 years and maybe they have plans for another five after that. Their fee for a single concert ranges between £800–£2000 (but as I write their fee is sure to be going up, ticking away with inflation like a taxi meter). This group includes Claudio Abbado, Daniel Barenboim, Pierre Boulez, Colin Davis, Bernard Haitink, James Levine, Carlos Kleiber, Rafael Kubelik, Lorin Maazel, Zubin Mehta, Riccardo Muti, Eugene Ormandy, Seiji Ozawa, André Previn and Rostropovich.

Then come the *one-star* men, excellent conductors, who may earn £400–£800 for a guest appearance: Sir Adrian Boult, Rafael Fruhbeck de Burgos, Celibadache, Antal Dorati, Eugen Jochum, Kondrashin, Leinsdorf, Rozhdestvensky, Wolfgang Sawallisch, Maxim Shostakovich, Edo de Waart.

When you read these figures, however, don't forget the hard work that is involved and the stress of being in the spotlight. A lot of the money goes in polishing the image, and in buying some privacy; then there is the expense of travelling, clothes and agents' fees—10% to 15% in the UK, higher in America (whereas Soviet artists receive not more than 10% of what they earn abroad, the State collars the rest). And, of course, income tax takes a heavy toll.

Nowadays, being one of the world's top conductors is big business; but, let's hope, never at the expense of the music.

Rehearsals

Kurt Goedicke is usually there first, setting out the various drumsticks on a piece of baize, and tuning his 'timps'. Then comes Renata Scheffel-Stein, the harpist, preceded by somebody carrying her instrument. The librarian, Henry Greenwood, is putting out the last of the orchestral parts; the string players sit two to a desk, sharing the same part which contains just their line of music; everybody else has a desk to himself because he (or she) alone is playing that particular part.

Two cellists unpack their instruments and examine each other's bow, looking along the length of it for some nicety of alignment; one of the oboe department opens a little metal box and starts looking at his reeds—usually there is one hanging from his mouth, like a cigarette; a trombone immediately brings out his newspaper, not sure if he is needed at this rehearsal for some time.

The strings play in everything, but, for example, most Mozart, Haydn and Beethoven works require only a few wind and brass; it's only when you come to the richer sounding music of the later 19th century, and after, that you nearly always need 'extras' like bass clarinet, cor anglais, double bassoon, big horn sections, full complement of trombones, harp and large percussion sections.

So in they come. No hearty greetings—these are men that meet every day, two or three times a day. No need for elaborate handshakes (unlike French orchestras where everybody shakes hands formally every day—it takes ten minutes at least). Sometimes the conductor gets there early and waits for the hour to approach; other maestros delay their entrance until the tuning is finished.

In the old days, when orchestras were much smaller, it was the responsibility of the leader to see that everyone was correctly tuned. Nowadays, the leader is in charge of the biggest section (the first violins) of the most numerous of the four families (strings, wind, brass, percussion) that make up the whole orchestra. He is the nearest to the podium, and so acts as the

link between orchestra and conductor. If the wind is being used, the oboe is reckoned to have the purest A, so before each rehearsal or concert the orchestra tunes to his A. Why A? It's convenient; all stringed instruments have an A string and the A that is used, the one above middle C, is on most other instruments.

10 o'clock. The conductor taps his desk with his baton. "Good morning, gentlemen, we'll start with Berlioz, please." He gives an up-beat and the music begins.

No two conductors conduct any piece quite the same way; and no two conductors rehearse the same way. But they will normally begin, if it's the first rehearsal for a concert, by playing through quite a good stretch of music. This gives the orchestra time to play itself in and to remember the piece; or if it's new to them, an idea of what they have to achieve, what to expect. Then, if there are a few things wrong, the conductor will go back, having mentally made a note of the details. "Let's take 4 bars before B, we must make sure these chords are together."

With his knowledge of the music and the entire score in front of him, the conductor can easily detect, when they play through that section at letter B, why it is that the chords are not sounding unanimous; so he is able to put it right and then move on. Sometimes he may want to get a drier sound, or he may want to change the tempo slightly, or he may want the strings to start a chord on a down-bow instead of an up-bow. Usually he will know what the difficulty is, but sometimes he will consult the leader.

Time goes by . . . coffee break. Each rehearsal is normally three hours long with a break of fifteen minutes at coffee or tea-time. (1-hour rehearsals are generally used to make sure of seating the orchestra correctly and to try out the balance of sound, plus any small points the conductor wants to underline.)

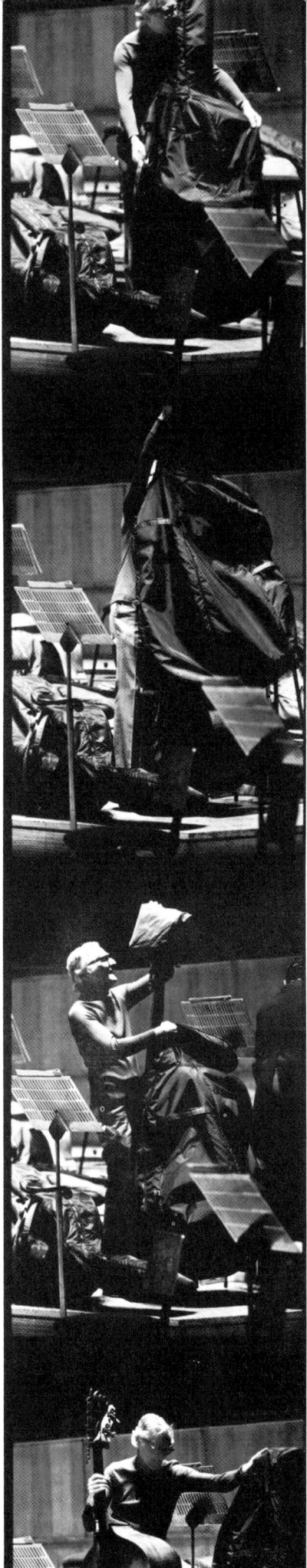

It is the orchestral or personnel manager's job to get rehearsals started and restarted on time. Lateness is usually criticised by the orchestra itself with a communal shuffling of feet. Even if a rehearsal starts late the union rules state that it must stop at the end of three hours. If the conductor is, or pretends to be, oblivious of the fact that he is about to sail into overtime, which may cost hundreds of pounds, then it is the leader's job to make him aware that time is up.

Once you begin to know the sound of the orchestra and its repertoire, it is almost more rewarding to attend rehearsals than concerts. This is where the work is really done, although of course a wise conductor will always store up something extra for the actual performance, otherwise the last rehearsal might be better than the concert.

It is interesting, too, to observe the relationship between the players and the conductor (and between the players themselves). Concentration is all important but then so is a fairly relaxed manner. Correction with a smile or a quip is much better than a barked command or a tantrum. An orchestra is quick to resent a time-waster, the conductor who talks too much or conceals ignorance, a man who gives up too easily, or one who tries to make a player look silly. The orchestra is usually kind to soloists and will applaud him or her on entry, and at the end of the rehearsal—unless they have performed very badly.

Sitting amongst the orchestra, the first thing that strikes you is the shocking din. That's not how it sounds on our hi-fi or from a seat about 50 rows back; but it's how it sounds to the orchestra and conductor.

To play in an orchestra means you've got to listen to the person next to you and to the band as a whole, or as much as you can. If you are in the strings, you have to get used to the fact that you can't hear yourself playing most of the time. If you sit in the violas, and the trombones are right behind you, you won't hear anything much if they are playing loudly. And if you are

The LSO in church.

in the woodwind, listening is almost as important as playing, because so often you are playing one note in a chord with other woodwind and if you blow too soon, too late, too soft, too loud, too much vibrato, too little vibrato, it is going to be noticed.

It's the same with the horns or trombones, where 3 or 4 note chords are the stock-in-trade, and you have to play as a team *within* the larger team of the orchestra.

Recently, the LSO and the London Philharmonic Orchestra got together and converted an unused church in South East London into a rehearsal hall. Until then neither orchestra had had a permanent place of its own. If they are not using it, then the other two self-governing orchestras, the Royal Philharmonic and New Philharmonia, can hire it; the BBC Symphony Orchestra has its own premises.

The LSO rehearsal room can also be used for recording sessions; it has a comfortable crypt downstairs fitted up as a restaurant and bar, serving good food and a decent coffee. An ideal place to relax.

But things aren't always so good for the orchestra. Most recording sessions, for example, are away from their home base, involving long hours, lots of travel, and, even worse, wretched food. During these sessions the orchestra is aiming at perfection for a record that is going to be listened to, and examined in detail, by conductor, colleagues, recording engineers and producers, public and critics. They can't afford to make mistakes because the sessions cost hundreds of pounds per hour. They're making music which is art, but somebody is footing the bill.

If one of them plays something wrong, messily, insensitively, or without intensity, he's holding everybody up. It may be a difficult passage, the lips get tired (brass), the reed is cracking up (woodwind), the shoulder or wrist hurts (strings), but *everyone* must be alert and sensitive to a dozen nuances, keep an eye on the conductor, remember what he's asked for, and what's been rehearsed.

In other words, musicians are playing on their nerves as well as their instruments, which is why bad food and bad coffee are no help.

Concerts

When you see an orchestra on stage at a concert, it has arrived there after a great deal of work has taken place. There have probably been 3 rehearsals of 3 hours each. Before that the programme has been discussed for quite some time: building a 2-hour scheme is not so easy as it may seem, certain practical and aesthetic considerations have to be chewed over (a delicate Mozart divertimento is going to sound at a disadvantage after some loud, richly scored piece like Mussorgsky's 'Pictures at an Exhibition'; likewise, if you need some out-of-the-way instrument to play just a dozen notes, it wouldn't make financial sense to put that piece in the middle of a Japanese tour).

Engaging a visiting conductor has also been the subject of much discussion and planning. The concert, or the series of which it is part, has been planned months, perhaps years, before; it is the subject of a brochure and posters, maybe magazine articles and radio publicity. Somebody has had to write the programme-notes on the various works, somebody has designed the advertising material; posters have been printed and billboarded in tube stations or other publicity sites.

Tickets have been printed, put on sale, sent out to critics who will review the concert in their newspapers. The conductor has been photographed at the airport or rehearsal, or given a television interview.

The music has been ordered, marked and edited; the piano hired and tuned (once before rehearsal, then again between rehearsal and concert; if the soloist is important enough, the tuner may even be standing by at the concert itself, in case anything goes wrong during the first half). All these details must be worked out in advance by the LSO staff.

Again Kurt Goedicke is there first, tuning his copper cauldrons, but this time he is in full evening dress; so is the rest of the orchestra as it drifts on. Should orchestras go to the expense of wearing such a formal outfit, even if the cost of it is tax-deductible? Most of the LSO think so: it makes it more of a show. And most of the repertoire comes from a time when people did wear evening dress. (Way-out, avant-garde music is different—T-shirts go with that quite well.)

If a concert begins at 8.00 p.m., the players will begin to turn up in the band-room any time after 7.00 p.m.—there may even be a few there already, players who live some way out of London perhaps, and are killing time. There's usually quite a hubbub of conversation, as well as tuning up, blowing down instruments, practising of runs and difficult passages. Some players will desperately seek a quiet place, so you might find a tuba in the 'loo' or a cellist in the boiler-room.

If Renata Scheffel-Stein is playing first harp that evening, she will go on to the platform 15 minutes before the start; but she is unlikely to beat Kurt Goedicke. Gradually others join them, woodwind carrying their instruments in flat cases, most other instruments 'naked'.

A conversational buzz from the audience; more tuning from the LSO, loud, then getting softer. On comes the leader, John Georgiadis. He bows to the audience, then turns to the oboe and everybody plays a final confirming A. On comes André Previn. Applause, more bows, and a handshake with the leader. And so another concert begins for the audience, another 'date' for the orchestra.

The music starts, and within a few seconds Previn is making that familiar swaying motion of his, a sort of shimmy; with his pointed nose and rather hunched up stance, his head seems to go straight down to his body without a neck. If one were to draw him, a triangle would be his shape. We are there to listen but, except for the dreamy eye-closers, we are there to look as well.

Is it better to have a conductor who throws himself about, giving a sort of mime of the piece, with gestures that try and express the content and emotions of the music (Leonard Bernstein is the supreme example of this school of conductors), or is it better to have one who just does what is necessary to direct the performance?

Well, let's face it, the players don't have time to look at all those gestures and, anyway, the shaping of the work has all, well nearly all, been done at rehearsals. In theory, it ought to be the conductor who gestures little (Rudolf Kempe of the BBC Symphony was a good example); but in practice, it does help the audience to have somebody point the way the music is going. Previn is about half-way between the two.

So there we sit, listening and enjoying and reading our programme notes in between the items; never thinking that, although tickets are getting dearer all the time, if the government and a sponsor were not subsidizing this concert heavily, it could not take place.

Records, Films & Television

A recording session is like a rehearsal and a concert jammed together. Except there is no audience; only several microphones, which are more sensitive and selective than humans, but less stimulating. There are humans however in the next room; recording engineers and producers, whose job it is to make sure that what comes through the wires on to the multi-track tapes will transfer properly on to long-playing records or cassettes. Clarity and perfection are the objectives.

When tapes were first invented the technique was to record a few bars, then the next few, and 'splice' them together. But then people realized that this recorded patchwork sounded unconvincing; so nowadays whole chunks, 10 minutes or more where possible, are recorded at a time. Sometimes a retake of a short passage or a single note is spliced into another 'take'. But union rules forbid the taping of more than 20 minutes of music at any one 3-hour session.

Recording film music.

'Rehearse and record' is the rule where gramophone records are concerned—'discontinuous recording' it is called in the television studios. While the orchestra rehearses, the engineers listen to make sure that the balance of the sound is all right; then a take is made. The conductor has a telephone hot-line through to the producer. "Let's do it again, fellows; watch out for the crescendo at letter D; the woodwind intonation was shaky at F; and side-drum, please look my way at G."

Another take. The hot-line squeaks affirmatively, at which the conductor and a handful of principals troop into the control room to listen to the playback of that take. The rest of the orchestra read, yawn, slip out for a smoke, or visit the lavatory. Recording is a waiting game. Still, it gives the lip, arm, or hands a rest.

Tiresome things happen. The horn plays his difficult solo like an angel—but a chair creaks. He tries it again—and cracks a top note. Yet another try; the hot-line interrupts: "Sorry, we've got a problem." Three minutes go by while the engineers work furiously in the control room. "O.K." Horn plays his solo like a *fallen* angel. Once again . . . recording is not the easy thing it sounds on the finished disc.

Recording with singers, especially opera, creates complications and a difficult scene. The singing area is marked out into squares of a few yards each, numbered with large letters. The singers move about from time to time, so as to give the stereo recording an impression of the action in the operatic story: exits and entrances, crowds approaching and departing, soprano and tenor changing position.

Film sessions pay well, which is some compensation for the boredom of playing music which is usually not as good as the concert repertoire. An additional frustration for the orchestra is that the movie is shown on a screen behind them, which means that they cannot see it although the conductor can.

For him, laying a music track is a hair-raising but exciting task: the musical 'take' is supposed to fit the visual film 'take'. What happens is that the conductor stands in front of the orchestra 'at the ready'. On the screen he sees first a countdown from 10, at the end of which the film sequence starts. Beside the screen is a clock marking the seconds. The conductor's job is to steer between the music, the film, and the clock. If he misses, they do it again. And again. And once again...

Again and again is a feature of the television session too. Boredom is another feature, because there are ten times more things that can go wrong in the studio. In the recording studio you wait during the playbacks; in the film studio you wait until the film is rewound; in the television studio you wait while they get the lighting, the sound, the camera angles, the boom, the decor, the effects, the make-up, and a dozen other details right. Of course the different techniques and technology can be interesting for the players, provided they don't do too many sessions of any one sort. And it can be fun wandering around the television studios and eating in the canteen cheek-by-jowl with some of the familiar faces from the small screen.

It is this variety that makes the LSO such a fascinating life: concerts with the world's top conductors, soloists and composers; tours in exciting places; occasional trips into the various studios. Sometimes at home the members of the orchestra can catch up with themselves by listening to their own records, and watching the LSO on television.

Recording music for a pop record.

Recruitment

Sometimes the playing of a member of the orchestra may deteriorate, or somebody behind him may improve. Promotions and demotions are tricky things to decide on; there is the pride and livelihood of the player to consider, but then there is the orchestra's good to consider first.

There have been upheavals in the LSO when several people have been fired or whole groups have resigned. At such times the personnel has changed considerably and quickly. But generally speaking, there are few vacancies, perhaps only one or two a year, when somebody retires or another gets offered a better job elsewhere. Members of the orchestra don't go in fear of their positions, not as a rule, although it does occasionally happen that a player may be cautioned if the majority opinion demands that a word should be said. With so many concerts and recordings, a weak link in the playing soon shows up.

Recruitment into the LSO works in two ways. The more senior positions are usually done by negotiation: a certain player, maybe in another orchestra, will be asked if he is interested in joining the LSO (obviously it would have to be a better position than the one he has already; or it might be that the player prefers the LSO to the orchestra he is in; or maybe he is playing out of town somewhere and wants to get to the capital).

Lesser positions, rank-and-file, are usually advertised in the newspapers. There is then an audition in front of a group from the orchestra, who act as the selection panel. The candidate is asked to play part of a concerto or solo of his own choice, something from an orchestral work or two, and to read some music at sight.

Those rank-and-file players lucky enough to be selected for the LSO will earn approximately £5000 a year. The principals get up to around £7000/£8000, with the leader of the orchestra receiving the highest fees of all.

Out of their income, the members of the orchestra have to try and maintain their delicate and expensive instruments. One example: it took Douglas Cummings, the LSO's brilliant young first cellist, three years to pay for his beautiful 1711 cello. The cost was around £5000, although it is worth more now. Insurance and maintenance add up to about £300 a year, and a good bow costs anything between £500/£1000. He also has to have a spare cello in reserve, in case anything happens to the number one instrument.

Unlike the other major London orchestras, the LSO has very few female players; in fact, just one. This, they claim, is not by design; it's just that women seldom audition for the LSO, and when they do, they rarely prove to be as good as the men putting in for the same job. Least, that's what they say!

No doubt the orchestra's playing will drown any cries of 'male chauvinism'.

The Orchestra

Looking around the LSO is much the same as looking around any of the world's major orchestras; different players of course (which is one of the reasons why no two orchestras ever sound exactly alike), but the same line-up of instruments—more or less, anyway.

At full strength the LSO numbers about 90 players. Let's start with the flutes.

There are three of them in the LSO, although the third usually plays the piccolo. Flutes can play slow and exotic, but more likely cool and agile; whereas the piccolo is higher, shriller and more flighty. Occasionally used, especially in really modern music, is the bigger, alto flute, lower sounding.

Flutes are frequently made of metal nowadays, although originally wood; if the metal is silver, gold or platinum, it's not to show off—it's tone they are after.

The oboe has a plaintive quality—it can do a pastoral jig but its natural sound is plangent. It is the thinnest sounding of the wind instruments. Unlike the flutes, the third member of the oboe section in an orchestra is not higher than its mates but lower, and is called the cor anglais or English horn. The flute is played sideways, the oboe straight down; the cor anglais has a curve in its mouthpiece.

The clarinet is a mellow instrument and fantastically mobile. Its range ventures down a bit into the bass, unlike the flutes and oboes which live up in the treble or soprano register (that is, except for the alto flute and cor anglais). The third member of the clarinet triad is the bass clarinet, which, as its name suggests, goes further down into the bass than any of them. Like the ordinary clarinets (each player needs a pair, one in B flat, one in A), the bass is adept at diminuendo (growing softer) and can disappear slowly like the smile of a Cheshire cat.

Clarinets gurgle well in the lower register, and the base is so sinister that if you should hear it in the soundtrack of a film, you can be sure somebody is about to get bumped off. Occasionally you might come across a smaller clarinet in E flat or D—ideal for depicting shrill or vulgar people.

In the orchestra, the third or bass clarinet is sometimes called upon to play the saxophone as well.

Remembering the story of 'Peter and the Wolf' (Prokofiev) where the flute was bird, oboe was duck, and clarinet was cat (all good casting), the bassoon played the grandfather. He is often also cast as funny man, a role he performs with good grace, although the one he *prefers* is that of romantic baritone—even though the accompaniment has to be thinned out, otherwise he won't be heard. Up in the high register the bassoon makes a weird and unearthly sound, perfect for the opening of Stravinsky's 'Rite of Spring'.

The bassoon is actually 9 feet long but its tubing is bent double; it has a long mouthpiece of darkly varnished maple. The second bassoon has a very responsible position, for he forms the bass of the woodwind choir; his intonation is important, second only to the tuba who is fundamental to the *whole* orchestra and, of course, very much louder than any bassoon. The contra or double bassoon is called for in many works from the mid-19th century onwards and is the third instrument in the section.

The flute and piccolo are the only woodwind instruments that require no reed. The simplest form of reed is a blade of grass, and the detachable reed on the clarinet or saxophone is simply a more sophisticated version of this, made of cane. Oboes and bassoons use two pieces of cane, joined together to make a tubular form at one end and a smaller, flatter opening at the other, through which the breath is applied. Woodwind players go through hundreds of reeds a year, some lasting only a day and few more than a week.

Woodwind instruments at one time were played as much out-of-doors as in—serenades in palace courtyards, and that sort of thing.

Brass instruments were meant to be heard from further away: summoning to battle (trumpet), to procession and pageantry (sackbuts, or their modern equivalent, trombones), or to the hunt (horns). Which is why trumpets and trombones especially have to tread carefully in the concert-hall; one of them by himself can make as much noise as sixteen fiddles. Some instruments can get away with 'coming in' wrong, but a trumpet is as diplomatic as a bull in a china shop.

The trumpet is noble and brilliant up top, doleful down below; when muted it can sound mysterious or jazzy. Horns, of course, are romantic when not in hunting roles; they are also intriguing to look at, curled like brass snails.

To play the little notes, like adjacent ones on a piano or accordion, woodwind players need keys; most brass players—trumpet, horns and tuba—need valves. Trombones, though, use slides, so that they can easily play between the notes (just as string players do) if they judge or mis-judge the distance. Like the bassoons, brass instruments would be a lot longer but for coiling up the metal inside them.

By the way, when you see brass players emptying their instruments of moisture, it is not, as you might think, 'spit' but condensation.

The tuba comes from the brass band and is really a kind of horn, but bigger and lower; the bass trombone can make a very loud, fat sound at the bottom, but the tuba can find such low notes more easily and more flexibly.

The normal brass strength in a symphony orchestra like the LSO is:

4 horns (plus a fifth who is a reserve known as a 'bumper-up' and not actually scored for by the composer)
2 or 3 trumpets (sometimes cornets are needed too, usually in French music—the tone is slightly different)
3 trombones (two tenor, one bass)
1 tuba (tubas vary in size from large to larger)

Fancy spending your life hitting things? If you do, watch the outer rim of the orchestral circle where the 'hit' men (the percussionists) live.

The copper cauldrons are kettledrums or timpani. Across the top of the cauldron is pig skin (vellum), and when hit with a stick it sounds higher or lower according to how tight the skin is pulled. The tightening always used to be done by taps around the edge; but composers came to like the sound of timpani so much, and used so many notes, that a mechanical method of tuning with pedals was invented.

The timpanist is head of his department and plays only kettledrums; he usually graduates from the rest of the percussion department, having worked his way up from number 2, 3 or 4.

The LSO has 3 percussion players and what they hit most are:

side drum (i.e. a drum small enough to be played sideways. Single blows on this are rare: the stock-in-trade is the roll—very difficult to play)
bass drum
cymbals (brass plates, a Turkish speciality)
triangle
gong, tambourine, castanets (Carmen's speciality, played on the move)

Except for the timpani, none of these instruments should produce a definite note; that is, no matter how soft or hard they are played, they make no note you could ever find on a guitar or a piano, or indeed on a number of percussion instruments which *do* produce a note of definite pitch, such as the xylophone, vibraphone, marimba, (and other instruments borrowed in the first place from jazz), and the glockenspiel.

There are dozens of other instruments, ancient and modern, that are being added to the percussion scene, which changes much more

than any other department in the orchestra. Things like crotales, whip (two bits of wood slapped together to sound like a whip—it only hurts if you get your fingers caught between them), bongos, boobams, cow bells, and many others.

Quite often these days a piano is used as part of the orchestral palette. The LSO keeps a player on the strength to play these parts which vary from 'scarcely-heard-but-you'd-notice-if-it-wasn't-there' to parts which are as difficult as any concerto (as in Stravinsky's 'Petrushka'). Robert Noble copes with all these and also plays the celesta, an instrument invented just in time for Tchaikovsky to use in his 'Nutcracker' ballet to characterize the Sugar-plum Fairy.

The harp is thought of sometimes as being lady-like—and is now often played by one in the LSO—but although it can be delicate, it is just as masculine as a cello or a flute (especially when compared with, say, the celesta). Perhaps it is better not to think of instruments as being masculine or feminine but as neither, as befits the harp which is, after all, played by angels.

Harpists in photographs or pictures are rarely seen using the pedals, invented in the 19th century so as to play all the notes of the scale; that is, the chromatic harp. In fact, the harpist uses the feet just as much as the hands, if less gracefully.

When the term 'string section' is used, the piano and the harp are not intended, although of course they belong to the family. The LSO strings are:

violins 16 *first violins, 14 seconds*
violas 12
cellos 10
double basses 8

These numbers are variable, but this is the strength the LSO keeps and it provides a satisfactory balance to the weight of the woodwind and brass. The strings are all members of the same family and are virtually the same instrument; but the violin can be tucked underneath a man's chin, whereas the bass is bigger than some of the men who play it. The viola is almost big enough to warrant being played between the legs like the violon cello, to give the larger instrument its full name.

Cellists tend to think of violinists as brilliant whizz-kids playing runny passages; violinists think of cellists as incurably romantic, playing their long, swan-like melodies and dreaming of fair ladies. Double-bass players think of themselves as somewhat neglected because they don't often get solos, but they know how important their task is: giving solidity and support to their nimbler colleagues.

The first violin of all is the leader of the orchestra. Next come the principals—the leaders of each section (first flute, first oboe etc.), the timpanist, and the third member in each section of wind and brass. The second player in each section (second flute etc.) is called a sub-principal. The LSO also accords principal and sub-principal status to second desk string players; but the men behind them, who have less responsibility, are known as 'rank-and-file'.

Just to confuse the picture even more, there are also some co-principals in the LSO to ease the burden placed on certain key players. Thus Osian Ellis and Renata Scheffel-Stein are co-principal harpists; so really one might say that there is only half a woman in the LSO!

London being a cosmopolitan place, it is not surprising to find that, as well as Welsh, Irish, Scots and Englishmen, there are representatives of Australia, Canada, Germany and Bulgaria among the players. A suitably mixed bag for one of the world's greatest orchestras.

Coda - A Sound Guide

A world-famous composer of our time who has made many records with the LSO is Benjamin Britten (recently created Lord Britten, the first musician ever to be made a peer of the realm). One record of particular interest in the context of this book is his work 'The Young Person's Guide to the Orchestra', conducted by Britten himself.

Britten (born 1913) wrote The Young Person's Guide to the form of Variations and Fugue on a theme by Henry Purcell (1659–1695). As well as being a great classic, the work is extremely ingenious in the way it is organized. First you hear Purcell's broad theme from the full orchestra, and then played by the various families within the orchestra: the woodwind, the brass, the strings, the percussion; then full orchestra again. After which come the variations which spotlight the single types of instrument—in turn:

> *Flutes, oboes, clarinets, bassoons (woodwind)*
> *Horns, trumpets, trombones and tuba (brass)*
> *Harp, violins, violas, cellos, double-basses (strings)*
> *Kettledrums, bass drum and cymbals, tambourine and triangle, sidedrum and chinese block, xylophone, castanets and gong, whip (percussion)*

And then comes the final fugue, the tune of which is the last of Britten's variations, played by all the instruments named above in the very same order; until at last, when all the instruments have come in and there is a big, general shindy going on, the brass enter with Henry Purcell's original tune, played at half-speed, while the rest of the orchestra continue to play Benjamin Britten's fugue full tilt. It is one of the great moments in all music—spine-tingling! Particularly ingenious is the way each variation has a mood very characteristic of each instrument—frisky flutes, plaintive oboes, and so on.

There is a more recent recording of 'The Young Person's Guide to the Orchestra', played by the LSO and conducted by André Previn (with 'Peter and the Wolf' on the flip-side, narrated by Mia Farrow). Either version would be an ideal companion to this book.

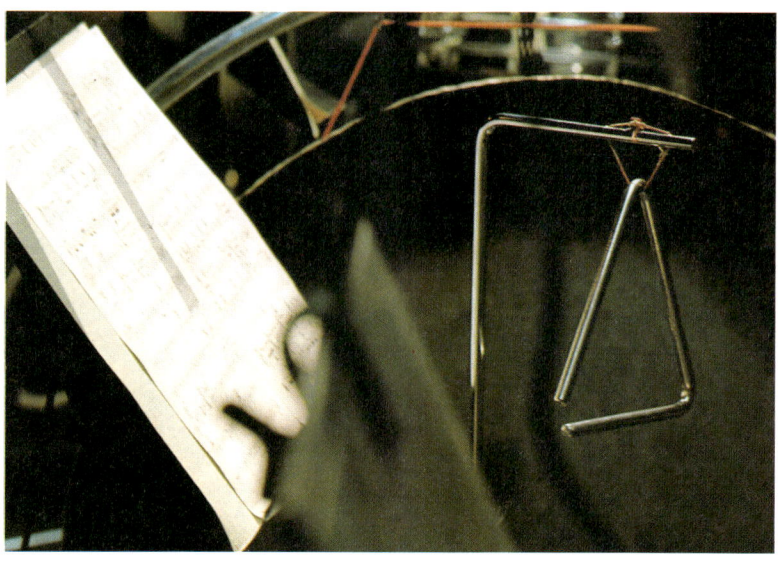

Cost of Instruments – a few examples:

Pedal Timpani: £800-£1500 (per pair)

Double-bass: £75-£800

Trombone: £100-£600

Cello: £300-£2000

Bassoon: £100-£750
Flute/oboe: £75-£500
Clarinet: £80-£350

Violin: £300-£2000
Viola: £200-£1500

Tuba: £250-£900

Harp: £1000-£4500

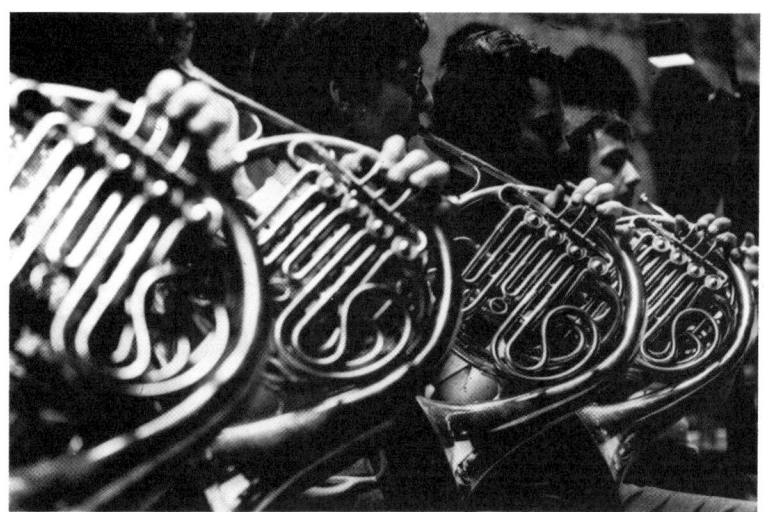

Horn: £150-£750

Trumpet: £75-£500

Note: the lower price is what a student or amateur might pay for a suitable instrument — the higher one is the *average* cost of the LSO instruments. On a recent LSO tour the instruments for the entire orchestra were insured for £250,000.

Glossary of Classical Music Terms

Avant-garde	*Experimental, way-out.*
Box	*(Orchestral slang) podium on which the conductor stands.*
Carve	*(Orchestral slang) to conduct.*
Classical	*Up to Beethoven (1770-1827), roughly.*
Definite pitch	*Sound that can be identified as to higher or lower, and even given a musical letter – C, D, E and so on.*
Fugue	*Piece of music or section in which the argument proceeds by means of a single phrase or melody, imitated at different pitches by various instruments or voices, so that you hear the same melody (or fugue subject) again and again; high, low, middle.*
Glockenspiel	*(German) play of bells; small tuned metal bars, played with sticks.*
Indefinite pitch	*Sound that cannot be identified in the form of definite pitch, like that of a triangle or bass drum.*
Leader	*The first of the first violins.*
Maestro	*(Italian) master, deferential term for conductor or important musician.*
Modern	*Stravinsky onward (1883-1971), roughly.*
Parts	*Each individual strand of the piece written out separately.*
Register	*Originally a term to sort out the high, middle and lower parts of the voice: head tones, chest tones and the mixture in the middle. Now one talks of the high register of the piccolo, the lower register of the bassoon, perhaps, or the middle register of the clarinet.*
Romantic	*Berlioz onward (1803-69), roughly.*
Score	*All the notes of an orchestral piece.*
Splice	*Joining two bits of tape together from different sections; i.e. editing.*
Take	*Transmission of sound to tape (originally of scene to film).*

Tempo	*(Italian.) Speed of a composition or its performance.*
The Brass	*Trumpets, horns, trombones, tuba.*
The Percussion	*Anything in the orchestra you hit (including the piano).*
The Strings	*Violins, violas, cellos, double-basses.*
The Woodwind	*Flutes, oboes, clarinets, bassoons.*
Timps	*Kettle-drums.*
Track	*Tape, or particular band on a record.*
Tune	*(Orchestral slang.) A work, piece of music of any length.*
Unison	*At the same pitch, all together.*

Douglas Cummings on his way to work.

factbook/LSO

The Publishers wish to thank The London Symphony Orchestra for their co-operation in producing this book.